Original title:
Wildwood Reverie

Copyright © 2025 Creative Arts Management OÜ
All rights reserved.

Author: Maxwell Donovan
ISBN HARDBACK: 978-1-80567-052-0
ISBN PAPERBACK: 978-1-80567-132-9

A Reverent Tribute to the Thicket

In the thicket, squirrels prance,
Chasing shadows, what a dance!
With acorns flying, tails in tow,
Who knew they could put on a show?

Beneath the branches, stumps abound,
Where fairies whisper, soft and sound.
Their giggles rise, a playful cheer,
While mushrooms nod, they can't stop here!

Twirling Dances in the Dappled Sun

In sunlit clearings, ferns will sway,
As rabbits host a cabaret.
With twirling hops and leaps so spry,
They're better dancers than I could try!

The daisies watch with vibrant glee,
As butterflies float, wild and free.
Though a bee forgets its dance routine,
Its fuzzy jig brightens the scene!

The Birds' Song Beyond the Bramble

Birds gather round for morning song,
Squawking loud, their tune's quite wrong.
A robin's out of tune today,
But who cares? They sing anyway!

Above the bramble, it's quite a sight,
Pecking and hopping with all their might.
If laughter could fly, they'd soar, you see,
With each chirp echoing their glee!

Temptation of the Untrodden Path

There's a path that leads to who-knows-where,
Lured by whispers in the warm air.
But watch your step, it's quite a tease,
A trip or two is sure to please!

With leaves that giggle, rocks that pout,
The journey there is full of doubt.
Yet every twist brings grin and glee,
Embrace the chaos, just let it be!

Symphony of the Unseen Lives

In the forest, squirrels prance with glee,
Bouncing about like they own the spree.
Chasing shadows, they're a silly sight,
Doing acrobatics, oh what delight!

Under the leaves, a snail takes a race,
With a speed that would put you in disgrace.
A rabbit hops by, laughing so loud,
As the snail just smiles, feeling quite proud!

The frogs hold concerts by the old pond,
Croaking and ribbiting—musicians beyond.
They sing for the crickets who dance on the side,
While the fish in the water just giggle, then hide.

A turtle walks slow, with a wink and a grin,
Says, "I'm just fashionably late to begin!"
The shadows all chuckle, the trees sway along,
In this quirky world, even roots hum a song.

Fluttering Pages of the Green World

Butterflies flutter like they own the page,
Wearing polka dots, acting like sage.
They tease the flowers to dance in the breeze,
While daisies chuckle, feeling quite at ease.

A bear in a cap tries to take a peek,
At bees organizing their buzzing peak.
"Oh dear, oh my!" says the bumblebee crew,
"Don't let him in, he'll want royal honey too!"

The trees reminisce about days long gone,
When falling leaves would dance at dawn.
"Be careful!" they whisper, "don't let it fall!"
As the wind blows through, it's a joyful call.

A porcupine struts with style and flair,
Dancing through brambles without any care.
With quills all a-twinkle like stars in the night,
He winks at a crow! What a comical sight!

The Secret Life of Leaves

In a breeze, they whisper tales,
Of sneaky squirrels with their trails.
They gossip about the sun's hot rays,
And hold court in the light of days.

With giggles, they twirl and spin,
Drawing laughs from critters thin.
A leaf once dropped, found quite the thrill,
With acorns giggling, 'What a chill!'

Flickering Lights in the Underbrush

Fireflies wink in clever rows,
Playing hide and seek, who knows?
With flicks and flashes, they prance about,
While owls hoot and dreamers doubt.

A rabbit winks with a toothy grin,
Says, 'Join us now, let the fun begin!'
In a dance of glow, they spin and twirl,
Awakening the night, giving it a whirl.

Embraced by the Emerald Realm

Mossy carpets, soft and bright,
Where toads croak in sheer delight.
Frogs in bow ties, quite a sight,
Sipping dew 'neath the pale moonlight.

They throw a bash for bugs and bees,
With cake made from the finest leaves.
Gather 'round, the show is grand,
In this sparkly, green wonderland!

Wanderlust Among the Ferns

Ferns wave hats as travelers stroll,
Whispering secrets, taking a toll.
With each step, laughter fills the air,
As snails race past, without a care.

The paths twist like a game of charades,
Mischievous gnomes with their escapades.
Singing tunes to tickle the ground,
In this forest, fun knows no bounds!

The Silhouette of Dusk in the Thicket

In the shadows, squirrels dance,
With nuts aplenty, they prance.
A rabbit hops with grand delight,
Chasing shadows, oh what a sight!

Fireflies wink in playful tease,
As crickets strum with crafty ease.
The trees lean in, they seem to chuckle,
At every flit and every shuffle.

An owl hoots with wise intent,
But even he can't help but pretend.
The thicket echoes with giggles and glee,
Nature's jesters, oh such folly!

As night descends with comical grace,
The forest wears a silly face.
A blend of chaos in moonlit hues,
Where mischief reigns and fun ensues.

Echoes of Celestial Harmony

Stars above begin to play,
Strumming night's soft cabaret.
The moonrolls in like a jolly guest,
To join the critters in their jest.

Bats swoop low with swooshing sound,
While owls share secrets they've found.
A raccoon giggles at the food,
That often puts him in a mood.

The gentle breeze joins in the fun,
As laughter ripples, two become one.
In harmony, the night is bright,
With every critter joining the light.

As dawn peeks in, the joke won't fade,
They'll hold their secrets, unafraid.
Echoes linger in the trees,
Of giggles and gags, whispers of ease.

The Untold Archives of the Forest Floor

There's a stash of tales beneath the ground,
Where mushrooms giggle and roots abound.
Old acorns hide secrets, round as they are,
While snails cruise by in their slimy car.

Underneath leaves, a dance unfolds,
With ants in suits, so shabbily bold.
A party hosted by tiny delights,
Where beetles roll logs in the moonlight.

Every twig holds stories untold,
A parrot squawks as he's feeling bold.
With every rustle and whisper, a laugh,
Nature's library captures the half.

Who knew the ground was such a place,
For capers and charm, and shadowy grace?
In the forest's embrace, all giggles stock,
A riotous library, tickles in the rock.

Veins of Twilight in the Canopy

Up high, the branches twist and sway,
Where squirrels flirt and boldly play.
In twilight's glow, a whisper shrouds,
As laughter spills from shrub to clouds.

Leaves giggle, tickled by the breeze,
Their secrets shared with joyful ease.
While shadows stretch, they play hide and seek,
In a game where only the brave sneak.

A raccoon peeks with curious eyes,
At a don't-tell-a-soul's secret prize.
Twilight's laughter rolls through the trees,
As the forest joins in with every breeze.

And as the stars begin to glimmer,
The canopy wears a whimsical shimmer.
With every chuckle, the night's alive,
In the arena where creatures thrive.

Interludes in the Meandering Stream

In a brook so narrow, a frog takes leap,
With a splash and a squawk, not a secret to keep.
Fish giggle and wiggle, all scales and fins,
While turtles in sun hats plot their wins.

A snail with a joke rides a leaf like a raft,
It quips about humor, delightfully daft.
The dragonfly dances, let's all take a look,
But who knew the fish had a thing for a book?

As bubbles are bursting, the laughter will flow,
Toadstools are giggling, where daisies might grow.
Underneath the sun, silly shadows play,
In this bustling dance, who needs a ballet?

With each merry ripple, more tales are unfurled,
Nature's a stage, in this whimsical world.
The stream, oh so lively, with humor infused,
In laughter like bubbles, we all feel bemused.

Where Ferns Tangle with Dreams

In the heart of the ferns, a squirrel tells tales,
Of acorns and mischief, and grand epic gales.
With a flip and a twitch, he swings on a new,
While the mice gather 'round for a laugh or two.

Dancing in moonlight, the shadows collide,
A raccoon in slippers now takes off in stride.
He stumbles on roots, giving everyone cheer,
As crickets pipe up, 'What a sight, my dear!'

While fireflies flicker, like stars dressed in jest,
They're buzzing a tune, oh, they know what's best.
A chipmunk sings loudly, with sass and with flair,
While the owls roll their eyes, slicked back in despair.

The magic of ferns wraps us all in delight,
In this tangled-up dream where the odd feels so right.
In the laughter of night, where all creatures teem,
A jolly good time flows like a fabulous dream.

Beneath the Veil of Stars

Under the glimmer of a twinkling sky,
A hedgehog in spectacles lets out a sly sigh.
He reads pies of comedy etched in the dirt,
While the worm tells a tale that's absurdly divert.

What happens at midnight when darkness does creep?
A bear in pajamas snores deep in his sleep.
But a rabbit in moonlight hops past with no care,
Trading gossip with owls, oh what a rich flair!

The stars overhear all the shenanigans spread,
As the night critters gather, the laughter is fed.
In this celestial circus, each creature finds glee,
With a coyote who howls out a bold symphony.

The dance of the woodland takes flight on the breeze,
While the night suggests games, if only you please.
In the glow of the stars, with each jest we share,
The woodland convenes with a whimsical air.

A Tapestry of Life in Motion

Among trees and tales, where the chaos collides,
A raccoon on roller skates whimsically glides.
The crows hold a contest for best acorn stash,
While the squirrels throw seeds, what a wild splash!

In this vibrant scene, a fox flips a pancake,
While badgers all cheer, 'Oh, for goodness' sake!'
With hats made of leaves, they host a grand show,
A dance-off begins, oh, what moves to bestow!

Each creature involved, from the wise to the spry,
Is giggling and rolling, giving forth a sly eye.
In a world color-drenched, so funny, so bright,
Life weaves its own quilt, showcasing delight.

So come join the frolic, in nature we'll clamor,
With tales intertwined like a cheeky-good glamour.
In the tapestry woven with threads all comical,
Every moment shared is simply ironical.

Verdant Secrets Unveiled

In glades where the squirrels scheme,
A frog croaks a noisy dream.
Mushrooms wear caps like hats,
While owls gossip 'bout the cats.

The trees whisper silly tales,
Of the time they chased their trails.
A rabbit hops in striped socks,
As raccoons play with cardboard box.

Beneath the bushes, ants conspire,
To build a kingdom on a tire.
Their little fortress made with pride,
While butterflies giggle and glide.

At dusk, the fireflies dance and blink,
In a waltz that makes you think.
What a riot, this green delight,
Nature's jesters in the night!

Song of the Wandering Breeze

The breeze plays tag with the leaves,
Ducking low, then soaring high eaves.
A tickled feather finds a nest,
While clouds frolic, never rest.

In shadows where shadows may creep,
The whispers give squirrels some peep.
A piñata made of pine cones,
Stirs laughter among the stones.

Chipmunks wear their brightest stripes,
Chewing nuts and swapping types.
The giggles from branches above,
Nurture bonds of forest love.

The wind hums a cheeky tune,
Bringing joy like a cartoon.
Indeed, the woods keep secrets warm,
Wrapped in nature's zigzag charm!

Sylvan Echoes of Solitude

In quiet corners, moonbeams tease,
Whispers float, as stars take ease.
An elf stumbles on some moss,
Trip and tumble, what a loss!

The crickets laugh in harmony,
As shadows stretch like spaghetti.
A shy raccoon in a top hat,
Hides behind an old chitchat.

The brook gurgles with a joke,
While willow trees begin to poke.
Sticks and stones join in the fun,
Even dusk knows how to run!

Each rustle carries laughter light,
In the forest's swirling delight.
Whimsical ants march, and parade,
In a world where giggles never fade!

The Forest's Gentle Lullaby

Beneath the canopy, branches sway,
A fox mimics a ballet play.
Leaves clap hands to the beat of night,
As twilight bursts in colors bright.

A sleepy bunny yawns with grace,
As fireflies join the winking race.
The starlit sky is a comic show,
Casting shadows where giggles flow.

The nighttime air, a tickle, a tease,
The moon chuckles through rustling trees.
Crickets chirp a lullaby sweet,
Bringing dreams for tiny feet.

And there, in the whispers of sleep,
Nature's secrets softly creep.
With each sigh of the gentle breeze,
The woods weave laughter, love, and ease!

The Spectrum of the Woodland's Heart

In leafy lanes, the squirrels dance,
They juggle acorns with a glance.
A robin sings a silly tune,
While mushrooms wear a hat like June.

The trees debate with wobbly roots,
On fashion tips from furry brutes.
A vine wraps round a sleepy snail,
And whispers secrets through the gale.

Critters giggle in the breeze,
As butterflies do pirouettes with ease.
The brook chuckles, splashing bright,
Reflecting joy from morning light.

Fragrance of Ancient Soil

The ground's alive with earthy jests,
As worms wear hats, their squirming quests.
A patch of daisies starts to cheer,
Their heads all bobbing, full of cheer.

The roots play tag beneath the ground,
While whispering leaves spin round and round.
Nuts grumble softly, feeling grand,
In this peculiar, nutty land.

Moles in tuxedos dig a hole,
Announcing grand, subterranean goals.
And if you listen close, you'll hear,
The forest grinning, year to year.

When Nature Paints the Sky

Clouds become creatures in the air,
With dragon shapes, beyond compare.
A sunbeam slips, a playful tease,
As colors swirl among the trees.

The horizon wears its wildest dress,
A patchwork quilt of happiness.
The stars poke fun with twinkling eyes,
As moonbeams giggle, low and high.

The dawn stretches wide with sleepy yawns,
As night wraps up its endless brawns.
In this amusing, painted view,
The sky's a canvas, fresh and new.

The Call of the Untamed Horizon

Beyond the hills where shadows leap,
Lies a land where yonder sheep
Wear knitted sweaters, oh so sweet,
While grasshoppers perform in beat.

The brook's a jester, splashing glee,
As frogs hold court beneath a tree.
Fluffy clouds pull silly pranks,
As flowers form their cheerful ranks.

A breeze comes dancing, swift and spry,
With tousled hair, it swoops on by.
In this silly, boundless place,
Nature winks, wearing a smiley face.

Sylphs in the Shimmering Glade

In the glade where sparkles play,
Sylphs dance in a quirky way.
They trip on twigs and giggle loud,
A merry, silly little crowd.

They twirl and spin beneath the trees,
Swatting bugs like summer bees.
With acorns flying, hats askew,
Their laughter echoes, ringing true.

By the pond where frogs do croak,
They tell their jokes with glee bespoke.
But when a breeze begins to blow,
Their skirts go flying, what a show!

With every slip and every fall,
They point and laugh, they heed the call.
In nature's jest, they find their play,
Creating memories for the day.

The Allure of Hidden Trails

On hidden trails where secrets lay,
The squirrels plot their games at play.
With cheeky grins, they dart and dash,
While munching acorns with a splash.

A weary hiker stops to stare,
As chipmunks dance without a care.
They flick their tails and jump with cheer,
"Come join us, human! Don't you fear?"

With messy trails through mud and leaves,
Each step a squish, he barely grieves.
For laughter swells in every nook,
As nature turns into a book.

With squirrels teaching him their way,
He learns to live, to dance, to play.
The simple joys of earthy trails,
Bring smiles with every trip that fails.

Chronicles of the Untamed Realm

In realms where only critters roar,
The tales of mischief never bore.
A raccoon stole a picnic spread,
And swore a lion had been fed.

Beneath the stars, the owls delight,
With whispers soft in moonlit night.
They gossip 'bout the deer's bad luck,
"Did you hear? She tripped on muck!"

The foxes plot schemes with sly grins,
While wild boar just snorts and spins.
They share their woes of thorns and brambles,
As laughter rings through wooded shambles.

With tales of treasure that goes awry,
Every creature gives it a try.
In life's grand play, they find their theme,
Finding humor in every dream.

Mysteries of the Whistling Pines

In the pines where whispers float,
A mystery wrapped in a coat.
The trees seem to gossip, trees seem to sing,
As shadows dance and the owls take wing.

But when the sun begins to dip,
And shadows start their evening trip,
The crickets chirp a curious tune,
While nighttime steals the afternoon.

What secrets hide in bark and bough?
The trees just chuckle, they won't say how.
A game of hide and seek unfolds,
As mischief and wonder start to mold.

So if you walk beneath the stars,
Watch for shadows and passing cars.
For in this place, fun hides in plain sight,
Through whispers and laughter, a joyful night.

Sunlit Pathways of the Heart

On a bright path where giggles collide,
Squirrels debate on the best way to hide.
A butterfly flutters, doing the cha-cha,
While a rabbit narrates tales of his mama.

Under big leaves, a parade of ants,
Conducting their business in tiny red pants.
They march with a song, all in a line,
Plotting mischief, oh so divine!

A frog wears a crown, thinks he's the king,
Croaks out orders, but can't really sing.
While the snails have a disco, moving so slow,
Their grooves are so cool, but can you feel the flow?

And as the sun dips low, what a sight to behold,
The trees tell stories, both funny and bold.
With laughter in the air, the heart's light as a feather,
In this silly woodland, all creatures are tethered.

Dancing Shadows Among the Trees

In the gentle moonlight, shadows prance,
A bear doing jazz, in a leafy romance.
The owls hoot along in their playful ways,
As the fireflies twinkle, setting the stage.

A raccoon with a top hat, so dapper and neat,
Sashays on a branch with a two-step beat.
While the fireflies buzz, lighting the scene,
In this quirky ballet, no one's too keen.

The bushes rustle, a troupe comes to play,
With a ticklish old fox leading the way.
Each turn and twist makes the branches shake,
Laughter erupts with each little break.

Between the tall trees, their shadows grow bold,
A chorus of critters, their antics unfold.
As night drapes its shawl, and the stars seem to wink,
In this playful forest, the fun's on the brink.

Breezes Carrying Forgotten Tales

Whispers travel on the friendly breeze,
A tale of a turtle who danced with ease.
His moves quite funky, his shell a bright hue,
Made the flowers giggle, all morning it's true.

The wind carries laughter, a memory so sweet,
Of a cat with a hat, and oversized feet.
He struts through the woods like he owns the place,
Leaving behind a trail of cake crumbs and grace.

A wandering mouse, with stories to spin,
Of sneaky cheese heists, and where they've been.
The breezes chuckle, as leaves join the fun,
In this light-hearted tale, everyone's won.

And when twilight falls, and the world starts to rest,
The breeze holds these tales, feeling ever so blessed.
With night wrapping gently, the fun's not yet done,
For in laughter's embrace, we all become one.

The Magic of the Mossy Grove

In a grove of green, where the moss grows thick,
A snail tells jokes, oh he's quite the trick!
With a tongue-in-cheek smile and a slimy flair,
His punchlines land softly like a warm evening air.

A curious fox with a penchant for cheese,
Mocks the old owl, who snores with great ease.
Together they giggle, a most unlikely pair,
In this magical grove, without a single care.

Twinkling mushrooms join in with glee,
Lighting the night like a party marquee.
While the whispers of wind croon a sweet song,
Each creature in sync, where they all belong.

As dawn peeks in, the laughter won't fade,
In this enchanted grove, where friendships are made.
With smiles all around, in their leafy cocoon,
The magic of joy wraps them all like a tune.

Brushed by the Hand of Nature

In the glade where squirrels prance,
Frogs wear hats, and dance a dance.
The bees write songs upon the breeze,
While plants plot mischief, oh what tease!

A chipmunk steals my sandwich bold,
While laughing leaves in shades of gold.
A flower sneezes, petals fly,
I laugh 'til tears, I can't deny!

The brook hums tunes that tickle toes,
With each splash, hilarity grows.
In a world where laughter reigns,
Nature's jokes driving us insane!

So come, dear friend, let's roam about,
In this forest, there's no doubt.
With nature's hand, we play and jest,
In a leafy land, we're feeling blessed!

Love Letters from the Forest Floor

The pine send notes with scents so sweet,
While mushrooms scribble, 'Do take a seat!'
Leaves rustle softly, whispering cheer,
Their messages loud for all to hear.

A dandelion's wish takes flight,
A ladybug writes, 'You're quite the sight!'
With twinkling eyes, they beckon near,
In this realm, there's nothing to fear.

Acorns giggle, bouncing in glee,
As each rock giggles, 'You're stuck with me!'
The forest floor holds tales galore,
Each step reveals love letters more.

With every brazen, leafy quip,
We dance and stumble, take a dip.
So gather 'round for fun letters found,
In nature's arms, laughter is crowned!

The Signature of the Elder Tree

An elder tree with bark all wise,
With doodles and jokes from ancient skies.
It's signature drawn with twigs and leaves,
A masterpiece that makes one believe.

Its branches twirl in playful forms,
As critters gather in all their swarms.
A raccoon winks, a fox thumbs its nose,
In this tree's shadow, humor grows.

Beneath its roots, we share our glee,
Telling tales that bounce like a bee.
A toad's critique, quite truly absurd,
Leaves us laughing, not even heard.

So let us bask in this silly rhyme,
With laughter echoing, a good time.
The elder tree's giggles fill the air,
In its presence, there's joy everywhere!

Recitals Underneath the Great Canopy

Gather 'round, for tales unfold,
Underneath this green so bold.
With ferns as fans, we take our seats,
As laughter dances in the beats.

A caterpillar recites with flair,
While ladybugs giggle, a playful pair.
In shadows deep, where secrets blend,
Each verse a chuckle, each act a friend.

A bumblebee buzzes, steals the scene,
With flower petals dressed so green.
A squirrel critiques with a cheeky grin,
"Do you really think that's how you spin?"

So shall we revel in this delight,
Under the stars, we share the night.
For under this canopy, so grand and wide,
We find joy in laughter—enjoy the ride!

Enchanted Echoes of the Sylvan Realm

In the forest, where trees dance,
Squirrels hold a daring prance.
They mock the birds with silly tweets,
Giving the mushrooms happy beats.

Beneath a bush, a rabbit snores,
While frogs plan plays on mossy floors.
The sunbeams stop for tea and cake,
Hoping the owls won't stay awake.

A fox in boots walks down the trail,
Winking at bees who tell a tale.
The leaves in laughter rustle and sway,
Making sure mischief's here to stay.

At twilight's edge, the twilight starts,
Boozy fireflies play their parts.
A nighttime ball where critters twirl,
In the realm where giggles swirl.

A Journey Through the Whimsical Woods.

Waltz through the woods, a trip so bright,
Where gnomes wear hats that shine at night.
They dance with acorns, spin and whirl,
As twinkling lights begin to swirl.

A raccoon plays a fiddle made of string,
While daisies join in some fancy sing.
They create a ruckus by the creek,
Tickling each other with laughter's peek.

Mice in jackets sip from tiny cups,
While chubby hedgehogs do the jumps.
The trees all giggle as branches sway,
Wands of whimsy lead the way!

Under the sky, secrets shall bloom,
Where spoons grow legs and brooms zoom zoom.
Round and round the fairies fly,
In this quirky world, we cannot lie!

Nature's Whispers

Listen closely, the trees confide,
The gossip of leaves and the cool river's glide.
"Did you see the bear's latest fashion?"
"Those polka-dot pants, oh, what a passion!"

A wise old owl, perched in his nook,
Winks at the clouds like a storybook.
He raises a toast with a crumpled leaf,
Celebrating nature without any grief.

The roots giggle beneath the ground,
As twisty vines tell jokes all around.
A snail might race, but it's quite a tease,
He stops for snacks, "Just one more cheese!"

Daylight fades in a cartoonish glow,
As shadows take shape in a funny show.
The woods turn silly as night draws near,
In this land of laughter, we hold dear.

Enchanted Grove Dreams

In a grove where capers unfold,
Mushrooms wear shoes when it's cold.
With every hop, the toads regale,
Each croak a note in a wobbly tale.

Pixies zoom with glittering grins,
Chasing their tails, oh, what silly spins!
Under a moon that chuckles so loud,
The stars join in from their fluffy cloud.

Beneath a tree with a cozy nook,
The squirrels read from an ancient book.
Yet every line is a playful jest,
Leaving all creatures in giggles blessed.

As dawn unfolds with a yawning hue,
All gather 'round for breakfast anew.
With pancakes flipping, the stories arise,
In this charming grove, where laughter flies.

Moonlit Embers in the Thicket

A squirrel danced on a branch so high,
Chasing fireflies that twinkled by.
He slipped and fell in a scruffy thud,
The glowbugs giggled in their luminous flood.

A raccoon rolled in leaves, quite a sight,
Wearing a hat made of mushrooms, just right.
He offered a mushroom, quite a fine gift,
Said, "A treat for the brave, give your taste buds a lift!"

The owl hooted loud, a wise sort of chap,
While foxes performed their own wild clap.
Twilight chuckled at the silly scene,
Where woodland creatures acted like kings and queens.

Under stars that winked with a twinkling jest,
The night in the thicket was at its best.
With every rustle and playful bark,
The moonlit embers ignited the park.

Shadows of the Ancient Boughs

In shadows deep, where secrets creep,
A beaver tried a dance, not missing a beat.
He slipped on a log, slid right in the pond,
As frogs croaked loudly, the laughter grew fond.

A turtle slow poked, with swagger so grand,
Proclaimed to the crowd, "I'll show you my band!"
But with every note, he just fell asleep,
While critters around him began to leap.

Beneath those tall trees, a picnic was spread,
With sandwiches stolen from a human bed.
Bunnies convened in a frenzy of munch,
As a badger chimed in, "I missed out on lunch!"

The sun dipped low, casting shadows long,
Echoes of laughter, a woodland song.
With every rustle, the woods held a grin,
In shadows of boughs, the fun would begin.

Echoes of a Tender Wilderness

A deer tried painting with berries and leaves,
'Twas abstract art, but no one believes.
A woodpecker giggled, said, "What's that mess?"
While squirrels debated, "Is this a new dress?"

A hedgehog rolled by, quite puffed up with pride,
Claimed he was dressed for the grand autumn ride.
But stumbled and tumbled, oh, what a sight,
Feeling quite foolish, he got back upright.

The nightingale sang, but forgot the tune,
While raccoons made beats on a hollowed-out moon.
They grooved under stars, making music so grand,
A flash mob of critters, a wild woodland band.

Through echoes of laughter, a rush of delight,
The tender scene wove a tapestry bright.
In wilderness tender, where joy found its place,
The wildlife grinned wide, in jubilant grace.

Beneath the Canopy's Embrace

Beneath the leaves, a bear joined the fun,
With a party hat made from a bun.
He danced round a tree, twirling with glee,
As chipmunks chimed in, "Come join the spree!"

An ancient oak watched, with branches wide,
As laughter erupted, no need to hide.
The raccoons served snacks from a stolen stash,
While the frogs ribbited, adding to the bash.

A pair of owls, in monotone hoots,
Critiqued the dance moves of all fuzzy roots.
"Too left-footed!" one whispered with flair,
While night critters giggled, utterly unaware.

As night wore on and stars took their place,
The canopy whispered, a warm, soft embrace.
In the heart of the woods, where silliness swayed,
Life was a party, unplotted parade.

Echoing the Heartbeat of Earth

In the grove where the squirrels dance,
Trees giggle as branches prance.
A rabbit chats with a beetle grand,
Debating who's the fastest in the land.

Mossy stones smile with a wink,
Whispering tales too wild to think.
Leaves clap hands to the wind's soft tune,
While mushrooms hold a secret moon.

Ants march by in a bustling line,
Reciting odes to their favorite brine.
A raccoon shows off his shiny loot,
Claiming it's the latest in woodland suit!

The earth chuckles with every beat,
From tiny feet to the deer's retreat.
Around the brook, the frogs croak loud,
Joining the laughter of nature's crowd.

The Palette of Changing Seasons

Spring's flowers wear a vibrant mask,
Bees buzz by, in quite the task.
A daffodil freckles the tulip's hue,
While the pansies gossip about skies so blue.

Summer bursts with the sun's gold rays,
Lizards lounging in a sun-drenched phase.
Frogs in shades of green and red,
Hosting a pool party at day's end.

Autumn whirls in with a crunching gown,
Leaves toss shade while the squirrels frown.
The pumpkins debate their spooky fate,
As scarecrows nap, feeling quite great.

Winter rolls in with a snowy coat,
Snowflakes glisten, like a glittering note.
The owls hoot jokes from high, wise peaks,
While critters snuggle in cozy creeks.

Through the Eyes of Roaming Creatures

A fox with swagger struts the path,
Cracking jokes to lighten the math.
Bunnies giggle at the puns he makes,
Wishing they too could join the pranks.

An owl surveys with a curious head,
Sharing tales of the stars in his bed.
Raccoons hold court, a bandit team,
Plotting brilliant heists, a wild dream.

The porcupine grins with quills so sharp,
Drawing doodles while singing a lark.
With every rustle, whispers are made,
As nature revels in its grand parade.

Chipmunks bounce with bags of snacks,
Hiding acorns like clever hacks.
A skunk politely clears the air,
As laughter spreads beyond compare.

Cradle of Forgotten Wisdom

By an ancient tree, secrets confer,
Roots entwined like whispers, they stir.
Mossy elders share tales untold,
Of days when the world was wild and bold.

A wise old turtle, with patience galore,
Winks knowingly, recounting folklore.
The wind carries stories, soft and sweet,
Of creatures brave and of wandering feet.

Beneath the shade, a lizard grins,
Dropping knowledge like it's old friends.
With every flick of its tiny tail,
Another riddle for the curious trail.

A hedgehog hums an ancient tune,
Mushrooms nod in the light of the moon.
Together they form a merry band,
Guardians of wisdom, across the land.

The Timbered Muse Awakens

In a forest where squirrels swear,
The owls gossip without a care.
Trees wear hats of twisted vine,
While pine cones craft a dance divine.

A deer tapped its hoof to a tune,
And raccoons held a midnight boon.
The wind whispers jokes to the brook,
Where fish wear ties, quite the charming nook.

Beneath the branches, shadows prance,
And mushrooms throw their own wild dance.
With every step, the trees might giggle,
As the sun sets, the fireflies wiggle.

Oh, what tales the woodlands weave,
In laughter's grasp, no one will grieve.
Tomorrow brings more silly sights,
In the heart of woods, where joy ignites.

Chronicles of Oak and Ash

Beneath the oak, a nut decides,
It wants to take adventurous rides.
It rolled away with quite a dash,
Trying to dodge a nearby splash.

A rabbit spun in funky ways,
While ants debated on their days.
They plotted courses underground,
Where treasures of breadcrumbs abound.

The wind teased squirrels with a riddle,
As the brook played an off-key fiddle.
Foxes pranced in their fuzzy suits,
And chatted about their pastry pursuits.

Even the shadows love to play,
In this charming, whiskered ballet.
With leaps and bounds, their stories clash,
Oh what fun in the oak and ash!

Secrets in the Shade

In the cool shade, a secret buzz,
A hedgehog hums and gives a fuzz.
With berries piled like hats on heads,
The critters plot while no one treads.

A snail declares, 'I'm quite the speed!'
As turtles roll their eyes and plead.
The grass whispers tales of days gone past,
Where shadows of laughter forever last.

A frog croaks jokes from lily pads,
While chipmunks wear their silliest fads.
The sun peeps through, with a cheeky grin,
In covert spots, laughter shall begin.

Beneath the boughs, mischief brews,
With whispers light as morning dew.
Secrets shared, they'll burst and play,
In the heart of life's cheeky bay.

Dreaming Beneath the Elderflower

Under blooms where scents entwine,
A squirrel dreams of some fine wine.
With petals soft, it wears a crown,
While bees around begin to frown.

A hedgehog writes its own best seller,
Its plot twist? A dancing feller!
All critters gather for the show,
Where laughter blooms and breezes flow.

The elderflower starts to sway,
A crazy dance at close of day.
Mice tap dance in tiny shoes,
As wildflowers whisper silly clues.

With stars above, a party blooms,
In joyful chaos, the laughter zooms.
Beneath sweet blooms, let's raise a cheer,
In dreams where fun is always near.

Forests Where the Fairies Play

In a lush green thicket, they take their flight,
Fairies with socks that are mismatched bright.
They dance with the squirrels and sing silly tunes,
While hiding from owls and dastardly raccoons.

Under a mushroom, a party they plan,
With acorn hats and a berry jam.
The air filled with giggles and slightly weird songs,
As they twirl through the trees, all the day long.

A fox in a vest joins the rowdy parade,
He juggles some berries, and seems quite afraid.
But the fairies, they're laughing, not a care in the world,
In the forests where their antics unfurled.

So if you wander through shadows and light,
Keep an ear open for laughter in flight.
In the heart of the woods where the fairies reside,
You might just find joy is the best thing to guide.

Lullabies in the Underbrush

In the underbrush, where the grass tends to sway,
Creatures hum tunes at the end of the day.
A hedgehog sings softly, with quite the bold thrill,
While a sleepy old turtle just takes a small chill.

Bunny's in pajamas, all snug and secure,
Dreaming of carrots, his heart is so pure.
While crickets compose tunes with a twist of their legs,
As the night wraps the forest, from limbs to dregs.

The leaves rustle gently, like whispers of fate,
While snoring raccoons waddle through the gate.
A wise old owl shushes the raucous squall,
And sings lullabies to all creatures, big and small.

So if sleep evades you, just take a short peek,
To the underbrush where the critters won't squeak.
You may catch a glimpse of the night's cuddly crew,
Lulling the forest to dreams bright and new.

The Enchantment of the Hidden Glade

In a hidden glade where the daisies bloom,
A wise old gopher is crafting a loom.
He stitches some laughter with threads made of light,
While ants wear their hats, and dance through the night.

The toads play a trumpet, each note quite absurd,
As a fox in a cloak recites the odd word.
The flowers all giggle, they wiggle and sway,
In a festival glorious, come join the display!

With every odd moment, new friendships ignite,
From the beaver who knits to the butterfly flight.
So bring all your quirks, leave your worries behind,
In the hidden glade, joy's the heart that you'll find.

For enchantment is real when you laugh with the trees,
And share silly secrets on the light breezes.
So tiptoe with whimsy, let imagination sail,
In this joyous mirth of the hidden glade tale.

Reflections in the Crystal Stream

At the edge of the stream, with a splash and a giggle,
Fish prank the frogs with their shimmering wiggle.
The water is clear, like a glassy delight,
Where even the shadows can't help but feel light.

A raccoon with a mirror checks out his new style,
With a crown made of twigs that he wears with a smile.
While ducks waddle by, quacking jokes that are old,
They laugh at the ripples, so silly and bold.

The turtles are sunning, a slow-paced parade,
Recounting bizarre tales from their froggy escapade.
While blossoms above steady watch from their thrones,
As the stream tells a story, a chorus of tones.

So come, gather 'round, let the laughter unfold,
By the crystal stream where the magic is told.
For when you reflect on the joy that's supreme,
You'll giggle with glee in this whimsical dream.

Moonlight Dances on the Ferns

In moonlight's glow, the ferns they sway,
A squirrel skids past, it's party day!
The fireflies flicker, a twinkling cheer,
While frogs croak songs that only we hear.

A raccoon arrives with a mask and a grin,
He steals the snacks, let the chaos begin!
With laughter and leaps, the night twists around,
As nature's jesters perform on the ground.

The owls spin tales of colorful lore,
Of how the big bear forgot what's in store.
They chuckle and hoot, as if they can see,
The shenanigans brewing, just wait and you'll see.

So dance with the shadows, let's join in the fun,
Under the moonlight, our antics begun.
For the woodland is ours, oh, what a delight,
We'll party till dawn, joyfully bright!

The Call of the Forgotten Pathways

Down twisted trails where mischief is found,
The lost little hedgehog rolls round and round!
The whispers of breezes invite us to roam,
While a gopher claims he's making a home.

A parade of fine ants march under the sun,
With tiny top hats, they're ready for fun!
But who's in charge? Is it the ant or the bee?
The debate gets louder, oh, can't they see?

A turtle's slow dance catches all eyes,
While rabbits gossip beneath the tall pines.
Each pathway murmurs a tale to be told,
Of critters and legends that never grow old.

When twilight descends, we'll gather and cheer,
For the songs of the woodlands are all that we hear.
With laughter and joy, we'll light up the night,
In the call of the pathways, everything feels right!

Tales from the Timbered Haven

In the timbered haven, the branches entwined,
The woodpeckers tap, with rhythm they grind.
A raccoon in boots leads a dance with a hat,
While chipmunks applaud, "Look at him, isn't that fat?"

With squirrels on stilts, they prance and they leap,
As the forest erupts in laughter, so deep!
The hedgehogs spin tales of their day on the run,
While porcupines chuckle, "Gee, this is fun!"

The whispers of pine trees sway in the breeze,
While fireflies waltz, like stars with such ease.
They twirl with the shadows, from dark into light,
Creating a buzz in this whimsical night.

So raise up a toast with the mushrooms so round,
To the laughter and joy in our timbered playground.
With secrets and stories, let the fun never cease,
In this haven we cherish, may joys increase!

Shadows of the Ancient Oak

Beneath the old oak where shadows play,
The critters conspire in a grand cabaret!
With tales of the moon and of grumpy old folks,
The laughter erupts from the wise little croaks.

A wise owl's riddle gets lost in translation,
While a badger's remarks spark hilarious elation.
"Who ordered the cheese?" whispers a sly fox,
In the circle of friends with their mismatched socks.

The branches above join in with a sway,
An audience eager for the grand play.
With acorns as seats, everyone cheered,
As the punchline of the joke suddenly appeared.

In shadows we revel, with glee in the air,
For the magic of laughter is beyond compare.
So gather, dear friends, let the stories unfold,
In the arms of the oak, we'll be forever bold!

Whispers of the Woodland Spirits

In the hush of leaves, a giggle flows,
As squirrels make bets on who eats the most.
Mushrooms wear hats, quite snug and neat,
While crickets throw parties, oh what a feat!

A raccoon in boots, he struts with flair,
Barking with laughter, he doesn't care.
Trees whisper secrets, each one a prank,
And all the beavers, they join in the flank.

The owls roll their eyes at all the noise,
As fireflies flicker like sparkly toys.
The pine cones chuckle, they've seen it all,
While the hedgehogs wiggle, having a ball!

From dawn to dusk, a whimsical scene,
In this woodland realm, where life's a routine.
Nature's comedians, dressed in green,
Hosting a circus, a trim and keen.

Fragments of a Forgotten Forest

In a shaded grove where the branches bend,
Lies a picnicking fox, with a feast to tend.
He spreads out his lunch, oh what a sight,
Chasing away birds that swoop in for a bite!

A stoat with a monocle reads the news,
While the rabbits gossip, sharing old ruse.
The trees all chuckle, their bark wears a grin,
As saplings attempt to dance in the wind.

Beneath the old oaks, mushrooms play chess,
With acorns as pawns in a fuzzy dress.
A frog tries to croak out a witty joke,
But slips on a leaf, oh what a bloke!

They gather to trade tales of the past,
With every new rumor, it's sure built to last.
Among giggles and gleams, under waning light,
The forest keeps secrets, all day and night.

The Serenade of Swaying Flora

A daisy prances with a poppy so bright,
While a dandelion sings to the moonlight.
Their petals flutter, in a dance so fine,
Spinning around like they're sipping wine!

Bamboo shakes hands with a willow tree,
"Would you like to sway more gracefully?"
It giggles and sways to a rhythm of cheer,
While butterflies flutter, drawing near.

The violets gossip with the wild thyme,
Their whispers entwine, oh how sublime!
But a clumsy bumblebee steals all the show,
And crashes headfirst, resulting in woe!

From roots to petals, the laughter runs deep,
It's a carnival of colors, where secrets creep.
In this floral soiree, let all join in,
With petals and giggles, let the fun begin!

Pathways Woven in Green Shadows

Down winding paths where shadows play,
The hedgehogs roll on this sunny day.
A turtle with swagger, moves like a boss,
With swagger so strong, he could be a toss.

The berries compete for the sweetest taste,
While a squirrel prepares for a nutty haste.
Chasing each other, they tumble and twirl,
In a race with nature, they flip and whirl.

The ferns wave hello to the passersby,
Cicadas croon tunes as clouds float high.
And when the sun sets, the shadows will gleam,
As the forest blooms forth in a whimsical dream.

So take a stroll where the laughter bounces,
Among the green shadows, where chaos pounces.
In these tangled lanes, hilarity reigns,
With every step, joy dances and gains.

Petals of the Twilight Meadow

In the meadow, daisies dance,
Squirrels steal a quick glance.
Bouncing bunnies hop along,
Singing softly, nature's song.

Crickets play their late-night tunes,
Underneath the smiling moons.
Butterflies with mismatched style,
Join the fun and laugh a while.

The grass whispers silly jokes,
Teasing frogs in silly cloaks.
A hedgehog grins with pointed pride,
As lively friends all gather wide.

Through the petals, giggles rise,
Underneath the twinkling skies.
Every creature, big and small,
Shares a laugh, they're having a ball.

A Symphony of Rustling Leaves

In the trees, a rustling sound,
Leaves are laughing all around.
A squirrel twirls, then takes a bow,
The wind shouts, "Hey, watch me now!"

A melody in branches sings,
As chipmunks wear their fancy blings.
Acorns roll like bowling balls,
And laughter echoes through the halls.

With every breeze, the branches sway,
As nature joins in on the play.
A robin jokes, a wise old crow,
The woodland party's all aglow.

A symphony of rustling cheer,
Bringing fun throughout the year.
In this concert of delight,
The forest shines with purest light.

Mysteries of the Untamed Hollow

In the hollow, shadows peek,
A fox with a funny streak.
Whispers swirl like autumn leaves,
Secrets that nobody believes.

A raccoon wearing polka dots,
Steals the snacks from picnic spots.
With giggles echoing down the glen,
The antics start, let's do it again!

The owls hoot, they write a play,
Plotting mischief for the day.
While fireflies glow, they flash their lights,
In this hollow, pure delight.

Every twist unveils a grin,
Join the fun, let laughter spin.
With nature's play, there's no more sorrow,
In this quaint and quirky hollow.

The Spirit of the Woodland Night

Under stars, the night takes flight,
Creatures gather, what a sight!
A hedgehog with a tiny hat,
Proclaims, "I'm the king of chat!"

A rabbit juggles shiny stones,
As crickets tap on their cellphones.
The owls hoot with a twist of fun,
Join the dance, don't be outdone!

The moonbeams laugh, tickling trees,
As whispers float on gentle breeze.
In the glade, the owls waltz,
Adding spark to woodland vaults.

With every rustle, tales unfold,
Of silly pranks and deeds bold.
The night is young, come join the flight,
In the spirit of pure delight.

A Reverie Amidst Nature's Embrace

In the woods where creatures play,
Squirrels dance and chase away.
A wise old owl looks quite bemused,
As rabbits hop, feeling confused.

The trees wear hats, made of moss,
While chipmunks argue who's the boss.
A bear hums tunes, with paw on hip,
As bees join in, a buzzing trip.

The sun peeks through, a golden glow,
As flowers gossip, soft and low.
They share the tales of bees' bad puns,
While shadows laugh, embracing fun.

In this mirthful glen, we roam too,
Where laughter grows, and woes are few.
Nature's jesters, in light we bask,
A joyful dance, no need to ask.

Where the River Whispers Secrets

By the river, fish flip and splash,
Sharing secrets in a dash.
A frog in shades croaks with delight,
While dragonflies zoom for their flight.

The water chuckles, tickling stones,
As turtles plot to steal the cones.
Willow branches sway with glee,
A choir of frogs sings in harmony.

Paddling ducks with a waddle so grand,
Discuss the gossip of the land.
Dancing leaves, a party begins,
In rippling waves where laughter spins.

So come my friend, take a seat there,
Join the river's whimsical air.
Nature's laughter flows like a stream,
In a place where joy reigns supreme.

Timeless Stories of the Leafy Realm

Under boughs, tales come alive,
Where ants hold court, and stories thrive.
The wind, a bard, shares silly lore,
As leaves whisper secrets, a playful score.

A hedgehog dons a leafy cap,
While fireflies enhance the map.
Mice gather 'round for a tale retold,
Of misadventures, both brave and bold.

Each flower sways, part of the jest,
As dandelions wear crowns, feeling blessed.
A picnic of laughter laid on the ground,
With sandwiches made from giggles abound.

Old trees nod, approving the fun,
While mushrooms join in, on the run.
This leafy realm, oh what a sight,
Where laughter and stories unite to ignite.

The Enigma of the Wandering Fern

A fern in shades of emerald green,
Wanders off with a cheeky sheen.
It tickles toes, a playful tease,
While bumblebees bow, as if to please.

With fronds outstretched, it takes a spin,
While squirrels chime in, a whimsy din.
A dance of shadows, swaying free,
Under the branches, pure jubilee.

The tales it tells of where it's been,
To ferns afar with a sly grin.
They giggle loud like siblings sweet,
In this grassy realm of merry feet.

So follow it, let joy take flight,
As leaves play tricks in the soft moonlight.
In the company of nature's cheer,
The wandering fern brings laughter near.

Starlit Pathways Through the Grove

Beneath the stars, the raccoons prance,
Chasing fireflies in a wild dance.
A squirrel in a hat, wearing a grin,
Says, "Join the party, let the fun begin!"

The moonlight shines on a funny bear,
Who tries to juggle, but flies in the air.
Leaves in a rustle, laughter so bright,
In this grove, we party all night!

A wise old owl hoots, "What a sight!"
As the brook giggles, sparkling and light.
With mushrooms as stools and pine cones as snacks,
We toast to the night, and the woodland antics!

So leap through the shadows, be merry and free,
Hang out with critters, just you wait and see.
For starlit fun and woodland cheer,
We'll dance till dawn, no need for fear!

Tides of Time in the Leafy Realm

In the leafy realm, where the laughter flows,
Time ticks in rhythms only nature knows.
A turtle in shades, acting quite sly,
Says, "Catch me if you can, but I'll just lie!"

The flowers cheekily sway to the beat,
While the winds play tag with their fragrant feet.
A deer wearing sneakers runs by with a laugh,
"Oh look, it's a jog, not an afterward bath!"

The clouds whisper gossip with the trees,
City squirrels scurry, aiming to tease.
The sun, with a grin, paints all in gold,
In jolly moments, this magic unfolds.

So let go the clock, take a joyful ride,
In this leafy realm, there's nothing to hide.
With breezes and giggles, laughter divine,
Time's merely a game on this lively vine!

Melodies upon the Woodland Stream

At the woodland stream, there's music in air,
Frogs wear tuxedos, what a comical pair!
Each croak a note, a silly old tune,
As turtles join in, under the moon.

The fish in their scales perform fancy dives,
While dragonflies dance, oh how anyone thrives!
A chipmunk grins wide, says, "Look at me,
I'm the maestro now, just wait and see!"

With reeds as their instruments, frogs take the stage,
While a beaver narrates like a wise, funny sage.
Oh, laughter and splashes, a bonkers parade,
In the heart of the forest, where memories are made.

So join the concert, leave worries behind,
In this stream of joy, true bliss you will find.
For melodies sweet in nature's embrace,
Bring smiles and laughter, a loving place!

The Whispering Oak's Secrets

An oak stands tall with a grin made of bark,
Whispers of secrets all after dark.
A raccoon with spectacles reads every line,
"No peeking!" he shouts, "This one's quite divine!"

The branches giggle as they sway in the breeze,
Sharing old tales, bringing shadows with ease.
A squirrel, half-asleep, on a branch starts to snore,
Dreaming of acorns, who could want more?

The wind flips the pages of stories untold,
While the owl shares wisdom, both sassy and bold.
"Gather around, for the tales will delight,
Of love, laughter, and silly old fright!"

So listen intently, let your spirit roam,
In the oak's cozy hug, find your way home.
For secrets of joy are shared with a wink,
In nature's own way, let's giggle and think!

The Language of the Pine

In whispers low, the branches sway,
They tease the winds, in comical play.
Pine cones drop like clumsy jokes,
Laughter rings from the shady oaks.

A squirrel scolds a passing crow,
With gestures wild, all for show.
They chatter on, the trees agree,
In nature's jest, we find glee.

The saplings giggle, bending low,
While ancient trunks just watch the show.
Bark-clad giants, they roll their eyes,
At leaves that dance and spin in guise.

So if you stroll where green things grow,
Listen close, hear what they know.
For in the woods, the pine trees shout,
Funny tales, without a doubt.

When the Nightingale Sings

Under moonlight, songs take flight,
A nightingale sings, what a delight!
The frogs join in, quite out of tune,
Croaking loud beneath the moon.

The owls hoot with a wise old grin,
As fireflies dance, their lights all spin.
The crickets laugh, they tap their feet,
In a concert of chirps, that can't be beat.

A raccoon claps with clever paws,
While deer prance, breaking nature's laws.
Together they weave a silly sound,
In the dark glade, where joy is found.

So heed the night, when the songbirds croon,
A symphony played beneath the moon.
For laughter echoes through the trees,
Where nightingale sings with utmost ease.

Sprites Beneath the Emerald Canopy

In the shade where shadows play,
Sprites are giggling, come what may.
They pull the grass, they tease the ferns,
With little laughs, the forest turns.

One sprightly sprite gets tangled tight,
In a web of leaves, what a sight!
The others snicker, they point and squeal,
As he wriggles free with comic zeal.

They race the brook with tiny feet,
Stumbling through, it's quite the feat.
With twinkling eyes and mischief bright,
They dance and romp till falls the night.

So if you stroll through forest fair,
Look close for sprites with wild hair.
For underneath each leafy bough,
Lies the laughter of nature's vow.

Dreams Woven with Moss and Light

In dreams where moss hugs the ground,
Funny visions swirl around.
A hedgehog juggles acorns bold,
As amber rays from trees behold.

A rabbit hops, with style and grace,
While a turtle joins the silly race.
They trade their hats, so odd and neat,
In a parade made of twigs and sleet.

The sunlight drips like honeyed gold,
On tales of wonders, forever told.
In laughter shared, as soft winds sigh,
Nature's canvas, oh, how it flies!

So dream along in this delightful nest,
Where moss and light weave zest on zest.
In every corner, a chuckle waits,
Bringing joy through forest gates.

Threads of Gold in the Green

In dappled light, the bugs conspire,
To steal the sun's most precious fire.
Napping deer with curious dreams,
Awake to giggles of mischievous beams.

The gnomes are plotting in a row,
To swap the carrots with a bow.
With glimmers of gold, they prance about,
Chasing shadows, laughing out loud.

A feathered hat on a passing toad,
Sets off a ruckus on the blooming road.
The hedgehogs waddle with fancy flair,
As dandelions dance in the warm summer air.

Twirling through fields with twinkling toes,
The bugs in suits, parade in rows.
Each stitch of laughter, a memory spun,
In the fabric of mirth, life's a playful run.

The Dance of Mischievous Squirrels

Squirrels twirl in acorn gowns,
Dancing quickly up the towns.
With twitching tails and silly leaps,
They tumble down in goofy heaps.

They chatter secrets, flop and spin,
A nutty world, let the fun begin!
With mischief brewing in every branch,
They plan their wily woodland dance.

Bouncing through the leafy skies,
With giggles caught in their playful lies.
Each somersault leads to a nutty find,
As laughter echoes, they're both sweet and unkind.

In the treetops, joy takes flight,
Squirrels chuckling till the night.
Their little antics, a jolly sight,
In the woodland's heart, pure delight.

Reverberations of the Grounded Heart

Beneath the roots, old tales unfold,
Whispers of laughter from centuries old.
A gopher grins with a toothy glee,
Sharing secrets as wide as the sea.

The owls are hooting their wise-cracked jokes,
While wise toads croak, like musically stoked.
The groundworms giggle in rhythmic sway,
Crafting beats in a wormy ballet.

A patched-up heart wrapped in leafy greens,
Hums the tune of nature's schemes.
With every step, there's a funny beat,
As the soil shakes with comedic feet.

In the quiet, the chuckles spark,
Grounded hearts dancing in the dark.
With every pulse, life's a hearty jest,
As laughter echoes, we feel so blessed.

Fables of the Rustic Orchard

In the orchard ripe, the apples play,
Telling stories in a jolly way.
With every crunch and juicy bite,
They laugh at woes, bringing pure delight.

The pears wear hats of leafy green,
Strutting in lines like they're the queen.
In robes of bloom, they start to sway,
Creating fables at the end of the day.

The bees join in, with buzz and hum,
Mixing legends, becoming quite the fun.
A wild jam session of fruits and bees,
Stirring laughter on a warm summer breeze.

In every branch, a tale unfolds,
Of giggles shared and friendships bold.
In the rustic orchard, life's a feast,
With every banana and nutty beast.

www.ingramcontent.com/pod-product-compliance
Ingram Content Group UK Ltd.
Pitfield, Milton Keynes, MK11 3LW, UK
UKHW021458280125
4335UKWH00035B/599